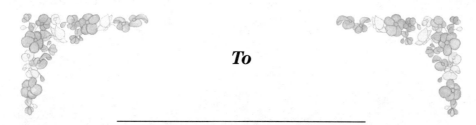

To

_____

From

_____

*Date*_____

Inspiration

The Helen Steiner Rice Foundation

Whatever the celebration, whatever the day, whatever the event, whatever the occasion, Helen Steiner Rice possessed the ability to express the appropriate feeling for that particular moment in time.

A happening became happier, a sentiment more sentimental, a memory more memorable because of her deep sensitivity to put into understandable language the emotion being experienced. Her positive attitude, her concern for others, and her love of God are identifiable threads woven into her life, her works . . . and even her death.

Prior to her passing, she established the HELEN STEINER RICE FOUNDATION, a nonprofit corporation whose purpose is to award grants to worthy charitable programs and aid the elderly, the needy, and the poor. In her lifetime, these were the individuals about whom Mrs. Rice was greatly concerned.

Royalties from the sale of this book will add to the financial capabilities of the HELEN STEINER RICE FOUNDATION. Each year this foundation presents grants to various qualified, worthwhile, and charitable programs. Because of her foresight, her caring, and her deep convictions, Helen Steiner Rice continues to touch a countless number of lives. Thank you for your assistance in helping to keep Helen's dream alive.

Virginia J. Ruehlmann, Administrator
The Helen Steiner Rice Foundation
Suite 2100, Atrium Two
221 East Fourth Street
Cincinnati, Ohio 45202

Inspiration

Verses by Helen Steiner Rice

Compiled by Virginia J. Ruehlmann

Illustrations by Samuel J. Butcher

Fleming H. Revell
A Division of Baker Book House
Grand Rapids, Michigan 49516

The endsheets,
enhanced with real flower petals,
ferns, and other botanicals,
are from
"The Petals Everlasting Collection"
manufactured by Permalin Products.

Text copyright 1993 by Helen Steiner Rice Foundation
Art copyright 1993 by PRECIOUS MOMENTS, Inc.

Published by Fleming H. Revell,
a division of Baker Book House
P.O. Box 6287, Grand Rapids, Michigan 49516-6287

Library of Congress Cataloging-in-Publication Data

Rice, Helen Steiner.
    Precious moments of inspiration / verses by Helen Steiner Rice ; compiled by Virginia J. Ruehlmann ; illustrations by Samuel J. Butcher.
        p.   cm.
    ISBN 0-8007-1692-2
    1. Christian poetry, American. I. Ruehlmann, Virginia J. II. Butcher, Samuel J.
(Samuel John), 1939–   . III. Title.
PS3568.I28P7444   1993
811'.54—dc20   93-12072

Printed in the United States of America

Contents

God,
open my eyes so I may see
and feel Your presence close to me.
Give me strength for my stumbling feet
as I battle the crowd on life's busy street.

And widen the vision of my unseeing eyes
so in passing faces I'll recognize
not just a stranger, unloved, and unknown,
but a friend with a heart that is much like my own.

Give me perception to make me aware
that scattered profusely on life's thoroughfare
are the best gifts of God that we daily pass by
as we look at the world
with an unseeing eye.

When troubles come
and things go wrong,
and days are cheerless
and nights are long,

14

we find it so easy
to give in to despair
by magnifying
the burdens we bear.

We add to our worries
by refusing to try
to look for the rainbow
in an overcast sky
And the blessing God sent
in a darkened disguise
our troubled hearts
fail to recognize.
Not knowing God sent it
not to distress us
but to strengthen our faith
and redeem us
and bless us.

Give us through the coming year
quietness of mind.
Teach us to be patient
and always to be kind.
Give us reassurance
when everything goes wrong

so our faith remains unfaltering
and our hope and courage strong.
And show us that in quietness
we can feel Your presence near
filling us with joy and peace
throughout the coming year.

*M*ost of the battles of life
are won
by looking beyond the clouds
to the sun.

And having the patience
to wait for the day
when the sun comes out
and the clouds
float away.

It's not fortune
or fame
or worldwide acclaim
that makes for
true greatness.

You'll find
it's the wonderful art
of teaching the heart
to always
be thoughtful
and kind.

25

*S*ometimes when faith is running low
and I cannot fathom why things are so
I walk alone among the flowers I grow
and learn the answers to all I would know.

For among my flowers
I have come to see
life's miracle
and its mystery.

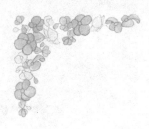

And standing in silence
and reverie
my faith
comes flooding back to me.

God,
grant me
courage
and hope
for every day.

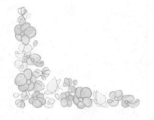

Faith
to guide me
along my way.

Understanding
and
wisdom, too.

And
grace
to accept
what life
gives me to do.

35

It's easy
to grow downhearted
when nothing
goes
your
way.

36

It's easy
to be discouraged
when you have
a
troublesome
day.

But trouble is only a challenge
to spur you on to achieve
the best that God has to offer
if you have the faith to believe!

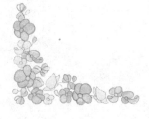

*L*ife is a highway
on which the years go by.
Sometimes
the road is
level.

Sometimes
the hills are
high.

But as we travel onward
to a future that's unknown
we can make each mile we travel
a
heavenly
stepping stone.

People
need
people
and
friends
need
friends.

And we all need love,
for a full life depends
not on vast riches
or great acclaim,
not on success
or on worldly fame,

but just in knowing
that someone cares
and holds us close
in their thoughts and prayers.

For only the knowledge
that we're understood
makes everyday living
feel wonderfully good.

And we rob ourselves
of life's greatest need
when we lock up our hearts
and fail to heed
the outstretched hand
reaching to find
a kindred spirit

whose heart and mind
are lonely and longing
to somehow share
our joys and sorrows

and to make us aware
that life's completeness
and richness depends
on the things we share
with our loved ones and friends.

God
is the master builder.
His plans are perfect and true.
And when He sends you sorrow,
it's part of His plan for you.
For all things work together
to complete the master plan.
And God up in His heaven
can see what's best
for man.

The silent stars
in timeless skies,

the wonderment
in children's eyes,

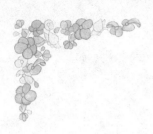

56

the autumn haze,
the breath of spring,
the chirping song
the crickets sing,
a rosebud
in a slender vase,
are all reflections
of
God's
grace.

$\mathcal{M}$y garden beautifies my yard
and adds fragrance to the air.

But it is also my cathedral
and my quiet place of prayer.

So little do we realize
that the glory and the power
of He who
made
the
universe
lies hidden in a flower.

The seasons swiftly come and go
and with them comes the thought
of all the various changes
that time in flight has brought.

But one thing never changes.
It remains the same forever.
God
truly loves
His children
and He
will forsake them
never!

It's not the things that can be bought
that are life's richest treasure.
It's just the little
heart gifts
that money cannot measure.
A cheerful smile,
a friendly word,
a sympathetic nod
are priceless little treasures
from the storehouse
of our God.